Summary: Mindfulness | Readtrepreneur Publishing: Includes Summary of Mindfulness & Summary of No-Drama Discipline

CW00469376

ABBEY BEATHAN

Legal & Disclaimer

Legal & Disclaimer

The information contained in this book is not designed to replace or take the place of any form of medicine or professional medical advice. The information in this book has been provided for educational and entertainment purposes only.

The information contained in this book has been compiled from sources deemed reliable, and it is accurate to the best of the Author's knowledge; however, the Author cannot guarantee its accuracy and validity and cannot be held liable for any errors or omissions. Changes are periodically made to this book. You must consult your doctor or get professional medical advice before using any of the suggested remedies, techniques, or information in this book. Images used in this book are not the same as of that of the actual book. This is a totally separate and different entity from that of the original book titled: "Mindfulness: An Eight-Week Plan for Finding Peace in a Frantic World".

Upon using the information contained in this book, you agree to hold harmless the Author from and against any damages, costs, and expenses, including any legal fees potentially resulting from the application of any of the information provided by this guide. This disclaimer applies to any damages or injury caused by the use and application, whether directly or indirectly, of any advice or information presented, whether for breach of contract, tort, negligence, personal injury, criminal intent, or under any other cause of action.

You agree to accept all risks of using the information presented inside this book. You need to consult a professional medical practitioner in order to ensure you are both able and healthy enough to participate in this program.

Table of Contents

The mindfulness program is flexible, and you can change it depending on your schedule. However, it is recommended that you practice doing it within the period of eight weeks to get the best benefits. If you follow the program, you will eventually find peace...... 17

The Book at a Glance

Practicing mindfulness has been the buzz lately in today's world. This is a good thing because many people feel the lack of some important elements in their lives. That being said, practicing the art of mindfulness is not just about being more present in life and becoming less judgmental to make things better. These are simply fleeting ideas that are rarely sustained. Living in the present and being less judgmental is a good practice, but this is only a part of a long journey to mindfulness.

Effective mindfulness must embody commitment and engagement from the person who wants to benefit from it. To put it simply, mindfulness is actually a constant practice. It is not merely a clever idea or a passing activity: it is a way of being.

The practice of being mindful has shown to give powerful effects on a person's health, happiness, and well-being. Since mindfulness is a practice, its development is a process that cultivates over time. It can be very effective if you allow yourself to commit strongly to the process. This commitment requires discipline combined with a little kindness and compassion to the self.

Having proper guidance is important when you go on the path to mindfulness, because your life and your interaction with other people could be at stake. Doing it in the wrong way could affect your mental balance, well-being, and happiness negatively.

In this book, you will learn how to develop the art of being mindful. Here you will learn a program that teaches you how to be more aware and observant of your own mind and body. Once you have finished the program, you will experience your life unfold and become ready for whatever comes your way.

Chapter 1: Chasing Your Tail

When was the last time you just laid in a bed without your rampant thoughts bothering you? Most people today can't seem to calm their minds and get some peace and quiet; lying in a bed to get some sleep could even be very difficult for some. You get that feeling that whatever you try to do, you just can't seem to shut your mind from thinking. You tell yourself not to worry about tomorrow, but then your mind suddenly starts enumerating countless things you must worry about. The later it gets, the more drained you feel. When the alarm goes off, you feel like you haven't slept at all and become ill-tempered and exhausted.

The following day, you experience the opposite – you want to keep yourself awake, but you can hardly keep your eyes open. You managed to get to work, but you just spaced out for the rest of the day. Your eyes were tired, your body ached, and your mind could not function well. You feel like it's taking an unusually long time for the day to go by, and you become more anxious the more time passes.

In this book, you will learn how to achieve peace and satisfaction even during your most stressful and troubled times. In a similar sense, this book will help you rediscover the feelings of contentment and serenity that are embedded inside you, no matter how lost and deep they are. These feelings are just waiting to come out from their cages: cages that you made yourself using your countless worries and frantic ways.

Many people nowadays have forgotten how it feels to live a life of happiness and goodness. Some have it even worse – they try really hard to feel happy that they end up forgetting what matters most in their lives, destroying the peace they were trying to find.

This book will guide you to understanding where genuine peace, contentment, and happiness can really be found and how you can find them for yourself. You will learn how you can slowly free yourself from stress, anxiety, and sadness. However, this does not promise a life of everlasting bliss, because it is normal to experience some sadness and pain once in a while. This book was made to make you feel a little less suffering and make you more positive about life.

The succeeding pages will provide some easy practices that you can add to your daily routine. These strategies were based on the work of Jon Kabat-Zinn called mindfulness-based cognitive therapy (MBCT) which was initially developed by John Teasdale, Zindel Segal, and this book's coauthor,

Professor Mark Williams. This method has been clinically tested and was shown to help people suffering from serious depression to recover. MBCT uses a technique that involves mindfulness meditation. This is a simple method that could help you feel the happiness in your life and prevent any prolonged feelings of sadness and stress.

A One-Minute Meditation

Sit straight on a chair and close your eyes. Focus your attention on your inhales and exhales without trying to alter them in any way. If your mind begins to wander, gently bring back your attention to your breath. After a minute, open your eyes.

Meditation usually consists of directing all your attention to your breath and how it flows in and out of your body. This way, you will be able to observe the thoughts that come into your mind, slowly, as you try to let go of them. Eventually, you will discover that thoughts can come and go as they please, and that you are not what your mind always thinks. Through meditation, you can be aware of how thoughts appear into your mind and then disappear right away. You then realize that your thoughts are transient — they come and go, and it is your choice how you would respond to them.

14

Being observant without being judgmental and being compassionate — that is mindfulness. Whenever you feel stressed or unhappy, instead of taking it personally, treat them like gray clouds in the sky, observing them as they slowly drift away. Essentially, mindfulness lets you become aware of negative thoughts before they greatly affect your actions. It helps you keep control of your life. Over time, mindfulness can help bring positive long-term changes in your mood and well-being.

Finding Peace in a Frantic World

It is normal for people's moods to change from time to time. However, some thoughts that can turn into long periods of stress and unhappiness. A sudden negative feeling could end up giving you a bad mood that could last the entire day.

Once you understand how your mind functions, you will realize why you feel down from time to time. It is normal to try to think of ways to get rid of the feeling of unhappiness. You try to figure out what it is that made you unhappy, and then think of ways to remedy it. Along the process, you could bring up past problems, which could lead to the build up of your worries. Your mood get even more grim and after a while, you begin to feel bad and start blaming yourself for what you're feeling. You soon start to lose your sense of rationality and begin to self-judge, finding fault in everything you do.

Many people get sucked into this quicksand of emotions because a person's state of mind is closely linked with memory. The human mind usually digs deep into the memory to echo the emotions that a person currently feels. For instance, if you feel scared, the mind digs for memories of the last time you were horrified so you will know how to react. This happens so quickly that you can rarely be aware of it happening.

This can also hold true for happiness, stress, and anxiety. Feeling unhappy from time to time is normal, but getting sucked into an endless cycle of negative emotions can lead to self-judgment. Eventually, they become difficult to stop and you drown in your sorrows.

You can't stop yourself from getting triggered by unhappy memories and judgmental thoughts, but you can stop yourself from falling into a spiral and attracting more negative thoughts. You can prevent these emotions from making you stressed and unhappy.

Mindfulness meditation will teach you to become aware when negative thoughts and memories arise. It reminds you that they are memories, that they are not real. Meditation helps you achieve mental clarity – making you see things with open-hearted awareness. It will take you off from the triggers that make you immediately react to things. Mindfulness does not get rid of the brain's natural way of solving problems, it simply gives you time to think of the best ways to deal with them. It will help you prevent your mind from drowning in all the noise and negativity. It will encourage you to be more compassionate and patient with yourself.

Happiness Awaits

Mindfulness works at two levels. First, you will be doing a set of daily meditations that you can do almost anywhere. Some could take only three minutes, while some would require you to spend at least twenty to thirty minutes.

Mindfulness allows you to break any unconscious habit that prevents you from living your life to the fullest. A lot of judgmental thoughts can arise from habits. By changing some of your regular routines, you could get rid of these negative thoughts and become more aware. You will be surprised by how happier you could become by making tiny changes in your daily life.

The mindfulness program is flexible, and you can change it depending on your schedule. However, it is recommended that you practice doing it within the period of eight weeks to get the best benefits. If you follow the program, you will eventually find peace.

Chapter 2: Why Do We Attack Ourselves?

Several people in the world are neither experiencing anxiety conditions or depression, yet they are not truly happy either. In life, people normally experience a change in mood or energy. One moment, you can feel very happy and content, and then other moment, you feel stressed and relentlessly pressured. You try to get a good night's sleep, but once you wake up, you don't feel refreshed at all. You begin to ask yourself how that happened to you — losing your happiness and having it replaced with distress.

Unhappiness, Stress, and Depression

Depression is starting to take its toll in today's world. The World Health Organizarion has estimated that cases of depression will become the second largest health burden worldwide by the year 2020. Chronic anxiety is also starting to become disturbingly common. The number of children and young people with anxiety has been increasing through the years.

Many people could experience downward spirals and easily snap out of them. However, some get sucked into the spiral until it reaches the point of clinical depression or anxiety. It is possible to step outside the troubles you are facing and free yourself from stress, unhappiness, exhaustion, and even anxiety and depression.

Our Troubled Minds

Your thoughts, bodily sensations, and raw feelings all make up your emotions. They act as some sort of background that is created when the mind starts to combine all your feelings, thoughts, impulses, and sensations in order to establish one state of mind. These different parts that make up emotions could tend to play off against each other and could enhance your overall mood.

It has been apparent how thoughts can drive a person's mood and emotions. However, in the 1980s, it became clear that moods can also drive our thoughts. This means that fleeting feelings of sadness can turn your thoughts into unhappy ones by changing the way you interpret the world.

Further research has discovered that it isn't just moods and thoughts that affect your well-being. It also involves your body. This is due to the fact that the mind is an important part of the body, and the two share common emotional information. A huge part of what the body feels is hugely affected by thoughts and emotions. It is a complex process that involves the exchange of information and feedback, but studies have also shown that the way people perceive and respond to things can be affected by slight changes in the body. Simple acts like frowning, changing your posture, or smiling, can make huge changes on your mood and thoughts.

Depressed Mood, Depressed Body

A study conducted by Psychologist Johannes Michalak and his colleagues examined the difference between how depressed people walk compared to non-depressed people by using an optical motion capture system. They discovered that people who were depressed walked slower and with lesser movement. They also found that they had a slumped posture when walking.

Try sitting with slumped shoulders for a minute. Notice how you feel while in that position. If you notice your mood worsen, shift to another posture, such as sitting upright. Now, notice how differently you feel.

When you see a person smiling, you could feel yourself almost smiling back. If you do smile, the other person will smile back at you, and you both end up reinforcing each other's happiness. It creates a virtuous circle.

However, an opposite, vicious circle could also occur. This happens when the "fight-or-flight" response is triggered. It occurs when you sense a certain type of danger or threat coming, and your mind tells you to fight back or run away. This could also be applied to the mind. A slight shift of your emotions could ruin your entire day. For example, if you feel stressed and unhappy, it can affect the way your body functions the whole day, making you more stressed and unhappy.

When you try to solve and get rid of any negative emotions, you activate a powerful tool in your mind: critical and rational thinking. It operates this way: if you find yourself in a negative state, and you know that you want to become more positive, your mind tries to bridge the gap between these two points. To do this, the mind activates the Doing mode. The Doing mode functions by subconsciously breaking your problems into pieces and are reanalyzes them to see how they can help you become closer to your goals. It works well when when you want to solve problems and get things done, but it has its own downsides.

Escaping the Vicious Cycle

The triggering of unhappy memories and negative thoughts cannot be stopped, but you can control how you respond to them. You can avoid the vicious circle from occurring and producing more negative thoughts. To do this, you must harness an alternative method of looking at yourself and your environment.

The mind does not simply think, just like how the Doing mode projects it to be. It is also possible for the mind to become aware of the fact that it is thinking. By allowing this pure awareness to occur, you will learn to experience life in a different way – unclouded by your feelings, emotions, and thoughts. You begin to see things in a different perspective.

Practicing pure awareness transcends your usual way of thinking. It helps you step outside all the negative thoughts and overactive emotions and impulses. It opens your eyes and lets you see the world at a different light. In addition, once you do, you will begin to feel a sense of contentment coming back to your life.

Chapter 3: Waking Up to the Life You Have

Experiencing your life at a different environment can help change the way you feel. Imagine yourself preparing for a much-deserved vacation. There were a lot of things you had to do and you felt like you don't have enough time to finish all of them. When you finally finished packing, you felt tired and had a difficult time sleeping because your mind was preoccupied by the things you've been doing earlier that day. The next day, you headed on to the beach together with your friends. You suddenly felt all your work priorities and worries slowly drifting away to the point where you begin to forget them at the moment. You feel refreshed and rejuvenated because your world has shifted its lenses. Of course, you still had work to do, but you were viewing it through a different place.

Time also alters the way you perceive life. Think about the last time you fought with a colleague or a random stranger. At that moment, you were enraged. A few hours after your argument, you began to think of all the things you could have said that would have made your arguments stronger. That argument probably made you feel bummed the entire day. However, after a few weeks, you got over it. You probably done even remember every detail of what happened anymore, and your irritation and anger had already disappeared. The argument still occurred, but you are now looking at it through a different point in time.

Perspective changing can greatly transform your outlook and experience in life. However, this can also raise a problem – these changes in perspective usually occur because something externally changed: you took a break outside of the city, or time simply passed. The problem is, if you depend too much on outside forces changing so that you can feel happy and new, you will have to wait for long periods of time. You constantly wait for a new day to come, for that weekend vacation, for time to pass. In addition, while you are waiting, you do not notice your actual life slowly slipping out of your hands.

Nevertheless, there is another way that can help you change perspective, internally. The human mind has its own way of relating with the world, called the Being mode. This is a shift of perspective that enables you to see how your mind distorts what you perceive as reality. The Being mode helps you to prevent your mind from constantly overthinking, overanalyzing, and overjudging. You will learn to become more aware of the world and be able to handle distress and difficulties from a different angle. You will learn to change your internal environment – your mindscape – no matter what is going on in your outside environment. Once you master this, you won't have to be reliant on external forces in order for you to achieve happiness and contentment. You will become more in control of your life. This is what mindfulness will teach you.

The seven characteristics of "Doing" and "Being" modes of minds

1. Automatic Pilot vs. Conscious Choice

Doing mode helps automate life by establishing habits. The downside is, these habits can eventually start functioning like an autopilot. You end up walking, eating, working, or thinking without being aware of the things that you are doing. Everything becomes a routine, a habit, until you start to miss out on a lot of things that are happening in your life.

Being mode — or mindful mode — helps you gain back full consciousness of your life. It gives you the ability to keep your life in check every now and then so that you will be able to make more meaningful choices and decisions. Learning to be more mindful will help realign your intentions and prevent you from wasting time over your habits.

2. Analyzing vs. Sensing

Doing mode requires analysis. Most people often function

through the Doing mode, to the point that you start to spend so much time inside your own head, unaware of the things going on around you. Today's busy world encourages more of this unawareness, forcing you to be buried in your thoughts rather than experiencing the world directly.

Being mode offers a new way of approaching the world. It's not simply about thinking differently. Mindfulness encourages you to get back to your senses, so that you can learn to bring attention to what is happening within you, and in the world, during every moment.

3. Striving vs. Accepting

Doing mode is full of comparison and judgment. It compares the real world to the world of your dreams. It tries to narrow the gap between these two worlds, making you end up with a toxic outlook in life that only accepts perfection.

On the other hand, Being mode teaches you to suspend judgment and self-criticism temporarily. You will learn to deal with things without preconceptions in order to avoid drawing preconceived conclusions that could limit your abilities and bring you down. Mindfulness acceptance allows you to acknowledge the things that are going on at the current moment, and helps you learn simply to observe these experiences rather than letting them control you. Through this, you prevent the vicious spiral from forming. Most importantly, it teaches you how to handle problems effectively.

4. Seeing Thoughts as Solid and Real vs. Treating Them as Mental Events

Doing mode utilizes the images and thoughts that it created as raw materials. This means that ideas serve as its currency, having their own values. Sometimes, you perceive these ideas as reality, which can become a problem in times when you're feeling stressed. You start to self-criticize and become unforgiving towards yourself.

Being mode teaches you that thoughts are just thoughts, and that you have power over them. They are not reality. Learning to recognize this sets you free from endless worries and gives you a clear path in life.

5. Avoidance vs. Approaching

Doing mode helps you solve your problems by keeping in mind all your goals and anti-goals. This can be a problem when it is used by the mind during times when you feel down and stressed. This is because apart from being currently stressed, your mind will try to bring up other feelings that you want to avoid, such as exhaustion or breakdown. This will only heighten your negative feelings. When the Doing mode is used at the wrong time and situation, it will only make you more exhausted and stressed.

Being mode encourages you to turn to the things that you are trying to avoid. It helps you approach these difficult states in a friendly. Mindfulness does not simply say "it will be okay" or "don't worry." Instead, it teaches you to face whatever feelings and emotions are bothering you.

6. Mental Time Travel vs. Remaining in the Present Moment

Memory and planning for the future are both essential for the functioning of your everyday life. However, these can also be affected by your current mood. When you are tired, you focus mostly on the bad things that happened to you and forget about the good. You start to think that bad things are just around the corner, waiting to happen in the future. You lose your sense of optimism and become unaware that your thoughts are merely past events or future plans. You become lost in mental time travel.

Being mode trains your mind to be in the present moment -- to see your thoughts as they are occurring, so that you can live in the present. This does not mean that you should forget about your past and future. The Being mode simply helps you see the past and present for what they are -- as memory, and as planning, respectively. Doing this will set you free from being controlled by mental time travel.

7. Depleting vs. Nourishing Activities

Aside from the possibility of getting trapped into autopilot, the Doing mode can also deplete your energies by getting caught up in all your goals for your life, career, and family. Having goals is good, but they can sometimes be too demanding until it makes you feel drained and affects your health.

Being mode helps you establish balance in your life by letting you distinguish the things that nourish you from those that deplete you physically and mentally. It will also help you deal with the unavoidable, draining aspects of life in a more skillfully.

Consciously Shifting Gear

Mindfulness meditation serves as an alarm that will awaken you when you are starting to space out from reality. It reminds you that you there's still a way out of the negativity that you feel. There are many possible alternatives to dealing with your thoughts.

The meditations that you will find in this book usually takes up about 20-30 minutes of your time every day, but the effects are lasting. You will eventually realize that even if some competition, comparison, and judgment is healthy, too much of it is unnecessary. A lot of choices that people make are actually false choices -- things that are driven by their thought stream -- and people can do away without them. You don't always have to compare your life with others, or with a fictitious life you pictured out for yourself. You don't need to be restless at night just because of overthinking about your performance at work earlier that day. Sometimes, simply accepting things as they are will make you feel more peaceful and fulfilled. If you really need to act on something, the best decision will come when you free your mind from worrying and overthinking.

Mindful acceptance does not imply apathy or resignation. It is not about being lazy or wasting your time doing nothing. Mindfulness helps you keep your life in check and lets you come to your senses. It allows you to approach the world in a calm and non-judgmental way. It helps you determine what is important from what isn't.

In the long run, practicing the Being mode will help you treat yourself and other people with compassion. It will give you a lasting type of happiness and change your outlook in life.

Chapter 4: Introducing the Eight-Week Mindfulness Program

The rest of the chapters in this book will show you how you can slowly settle your mind and channel your inner happiness through mindfulness meditation. The remaining chapters features two parts. The first part will require you to do a meditation that could last for up to thirty minutes per day. The second part is called "Habit Releaser", which helps you break out of your normal routine. Habit Releasers are tailored in a way that could spark curiosity and allow you to explore new ways of dealing with things mindfully.

Ideally, each meditation practice must be done six times in a week, once a day. However, you can adjust it to fit your schedule. What is important is that you finish the program so that you can get the maximum benefits that mindfulness is supposed to give you.

Setting up a Time and Space for Meditation

Before you start your mindfulness journey, you must first spend some time to condition yourself. The best way to do this program is to reserve a period of eight weeks where you can commit yourself to doing meditations and other practices. As you progress in the program, you will learn new practices that can deepen your awareness towards yourself and the world.

It is important to take your time and to follow the instructions even if you start to feel bored or think that an activity is difficult. Try to look at these practices as a way for self-improvement. The intention is not to strive for a certain goal. Happiness, peace, relaxation, and contentment are all by-products of the practices that you will be doing. These ones are not goals that you must pressure yourself to achieve.

How can you be able to set aside some time every day for your practice?

First, look at it as a way for you to spend time with yourself. In the beginning, you might find it difficult to spare a few minutes to meditate. You might need to readjust some parts of your life in order to commit to the program. You might need to wake up an hour earlier, but it will all be worth it in the end.

Second, when doing the practices, be sure that you are comfortable. Don't stay in a place full of distractions, such as the ringing of your telephone or the buzz from email notifications. In case anything distracts you, experiment by letting the ideas flow to your mind instead of immediately responding to what distracted you.

Finally, keep in mind that you don't have to find every practice enjoyable. Follow the practices daily until you get used to doing them. Every practice will have a different effect on different people and what they are going through. Each outcome of the practice is unique to the person doing it.

Chapter 5: Mindfulness Week One: Waking Up to the Autopilot

It is common for many people to become swallowed in their own busyness. This can have extremely powerful side effects, and could let the autopilot fully control you.

Autopilot can be helpful in extending the workings in your memory, which develop habits. Repetitively doing things enables the mind to link together all the necessary actions to accomplish a task with ease. This has allowed people to function and do complex activities at a reasonable amount of time. However, the autopilot also has its downsides, as mentioned previously. It can take full control over you if you do not know how to control it. Once you learn to be fully aware, you can be more in control of your autopilot and use it to bring out habits only when you need them.

Mindfulness of the Body and Breath

This meditation is designed to help you settle yourself in the present by doing simple breath and body movements.

Begin by staying at a comfortable position. You can either lie down on a mat or sit firm on your back on a chair. If you are

34

sitting, let your feet lay flat on the floor, and let your spine be straight. If you are lying on the floor, uncross your legs, let your feet fall away from each other, and let your arms lie at your side. Avoid being too stiff. Staying in the right posture helps bring you to your intentions for this practice, to be awake and aware.

Now, lower your gaze or close your eyes. Bring your awareness to your bodily sensations, and spend a few moments exploring them. Next, put all your attention to your feet. Focus on the physical sensations on your toes, your soles, your heels, tops of the feet, and ankles. Notice how these sensations arise and disappear. If you do not experience any sensations, then allow it to be that way. This practice is not trying to let sensations happen, it is simply becoming aware of what you attend to.

Now, move your attention to your entire legs. Notice any physical sensations you come across. Then, expand your focus up to your body --- to your pelvis, hips, lower back, and lower abdomen. Expand it further upward to your torso – your chest, your back, up to the shoulders.

Next, expand your attention even further to your arms, your neck, your face, and your head – bringing awareness into your entire body. Allow your entire body along with its sensations to stay the way they are. You do not have to control or change anything, just let the sensations appear and dissolve.

After a few moments, bring your focus to the center of your body, and start to become fully aware of the sensations as you take your inhales and your exhales. You can put your hand on your abdomen and let it sit the for awhile to feel your abdomen rise and fall. Stay here for a few moments. Again, do not try to control anything. Let the breath go through its own rhythm, let your body feel every sensation.

As you lay further in the practice, you will probably notice your mind wandering away from your breath. When this starts to happen, you do not need to rush yourself back into focusing on your breath. Take your time, allow yourself to sink in how the mind wandered. When you are ready, slowly, and with control, bring your focus back to your breath.

Continue doing this practice by yourself, focusing on your breath. When your mind starts to wander, allow the breath to ground you to the present. Always remember that the breath is always there to guide you whenever you lose control of your life. This is why a lot of people suggest that you take deep breaths during difficult situations in order to stay calm.

Do this practice at least twice a day for the first week of the mindfulness program.

Habit Releaser: Changing Chairs

For the first week, try to notice which chairs you would usually sit on in your house or at work. Now, deliberately choose to sit on a different chair, or alter the position of the chair you usually use.

People tend to become so used to doing the same things that it reaches the point where these things start to become unnoticed or taken for granted. It's surprising how easily people can stop noticing the sights, smells, and sounds in their environment, including the touch of a chair they are used to sitting on. This week, notice how you change perspective just by changing your chair.

Chapter 6: Mindfulness Week Two: Keeping the Body in Mind

The body can be very sensitive to even the slightest flicker of emotion that goes through the mind. Once it detects your thoughts, your body reacts to them immediately by responding to it as if they are real, regardless of whether or not they accurately reflect the real world.

Many people spend so much of their time in their heads that they forget about bodies, and how it can influence thought, feelings, and behavior. The tendency to ignore the body could be because a lot of people do not appreciate their own bodies – they are not as tall, thin, or attractive as they want to be. This could lead to totally ignoring the body, or mistreating it by ignoring the messages it is trying to send to the mind. Tuning out these messages from the body will only create more distress in your life.

By promoting oneness of the mind and body, you are able to synchronize your thoughts and your actions. In order to bring peace in your life, you must learn to come home to yourself, to the body you have taken for granted or ignored. Cultivating mindfulness encourages your full integration with your body.

Body Scan Meditation

Lie down on a mat, a bed, or anything else where you feel comfortable. Close your eyes, and let your hands lie at the sides of your body. Let your feet fall away from each other. Notice the bodily sensations you feel while you are lying down.

This practice is intended to allow you to spend more time with every part of your body and become more aware of it. Avoid any judgments towards yourself, and avoid trying to control your anything during this practice. Allow things to come to you naturally.

In this meditation practice, simply follow the instructions in the body and breath and as best you can, but this time, put more awareness to your entire body as you take your inhales and exhales. Whenever the mind wanders away, as it will tend to do, bring it back, without giving yourself a hard time.

Habit Releaser: Going for a Walk

Aside from being a good form of exercise, walking can also be an excellent mood booster and stress reliever. It's amazing how a short walk can actually change the way you perceive things.

For your first week, try to go for at least one 15-30-minute walk. You don't have to do this in some place special. You can try this practice by walking in a nearby park or in your neighborhood. When doing this, you don't have to rush yourself. This practice is not trying to make you reach a number of steps at a certain amount of time.

What this practice is trying to teach you is to become as mindful as you can while walking, by bringing awareness to your feet as it rises and as it steps on the ground. Aside from paying attention to your body, also try to be aware of your environment. Pay attention to the sights, sounds, and smells of everything around you.

Chapter 7: Mindfulness Week Three: The Mouse in the Maze

When doing something, the spirit in which you do it is equally important as the act itself. If you do something in a negative way, you start to activate your mind's aversion system, which can narrow your life's focus. You become less flexible, less creative, and more anxious. However, if you do things with a more open heart and better enthusiasm, you will be able to change the way your mind approaches things.

Three-Minute Breathing Space Meditation

Step 1: Becoming aware

Sit straight on a chair, or stand tall. Close your eyes if this feels comfortable to you. Take your awareness into your inner feelings and experiences and acknowledge them. Ask yourself, "What am I feeling right now? What thoughts are in my mind? What sensations am I having right now?"

Step 2: Gathering and focusing attention

Now, focus your attention in a more specific area – on the sensations of your breath on your abdomen. Notice how it expands as you inhale, and how it falls back as you exhale.

Continue to bring your focus to your breath, and use this moment as an opportunity for you to be in the present. If your mind starts to wander, gently bring your focus back into your breath.

Step 3: Expanding attention

For the last part of this practice, widen the field of your focus by including a sense of awareness to your entire body – your posture, your facial expressions. Imagine that your entire body is breathing. If you notice any tension or feelings of discomfort, take your focus into that feeling and imagine your breath moving around those sensations. By doing this, you are acknowledging the sensations and befriending them, instead of trying to get rid of them or changing them.

Habit Releaser: Valuing the Television

Watching TV can easily become a habit and be taken for granted. A lot of people come home from school or work and automatically sit down, grab the TV remote, turn on the TV, and start watching some shows. You start watching one show, and then another, and another, until you get stuck on the sofa doing only one thing – watching the TV. You know that you can do other more interesting things, but you just can't seem to get up and do them. You then start to criticize yourself – your posture while sitting on the sofa, your laziness for being stuck there, watching the TV, being unproductive.

This week, try to make watching TV a more valuable experience. For at least one day this week, try setting up a weekly TV schedule, and pick shows that you are really interested to watch. Make sure to follow your schedule, and only watch the specific shows you planned to see on the designated day. When the show is done, consciously turn off your TV and do something else while waiting for the next show on your schedule to come up. You can do a little cleaning in your house, read a book, or do a short meditation.

At the end of your day, write down in a notebook how this practice went. How did you feel? What thoughts went up while you were consciously turning off the TV? What sensations came up? Keep in mind that the intention for this practice is to help you get rid of old habits that have been deeply embedded into your daily life, so don't expect any huge changes immediately. You might discover that there are no changes that needs to be done in what you do daily, but you will learn to do these very same things in a different way – by putting more awareness into doing them.

Chapter 8: Mindfulness Week Four: Moving Beyond the Rumor Mill

The way you interpret and perceive yourself and the world can make a great impact to the way you react. This is what some experts would call the ABC model for emotions. A is the actual situation, B is how people interpret the scene, and C is how people react to it – their sensations, emotions, and impulses.

Most of the time, people are aware of doing both A and C, but are unaware of B. People usually think that the situation itself is what aroused certain emotions and feelings, but it is actually an individual's interpretation of a certain even that led to these emotions.

Imagine the world as a film where you create your own commentaries. This is what B is – your commentaries of certain scene. The thing is, these commentaries, which provide an explanation of what's going on happen very fast that you start to take it as part of the original film. Now, it becomes more difficult for you to distinguish real facts from interpretation.

Interpretations by the mind can sometimes act like a rumor.

They could either be true, partially true, or completely wrong. The mind finds it difficult to determine the difference between reality and fiction, especially when it has already started constructing a mental picture of the world. Because of this, rumors can tend to have power over your mind.

Sounds and Thoughts Meditation

Begin by sitting down, giving focus on your posture. Stay there for a few moments and start bringing your attention to your breath and body.

Now, start to direct your focus to your hearing. Be aware of all the sounds around you. Notice if your body starts to label any of these sounds as you hear them. Notice how easily these sounds can make stories in your mind. Once you notice this, try to bring back your attention to the sounds themselves, and listen to them just as they are, instead of trying to interpret them.

Next, try to listen to the rawness of the sounds – their loudness, rhythm, or pitch. Some sounds can be easily overpowered by other louder sounds. Try to notice them. Now, try to focus more and see if you can be aware of the space in which these sounds arise. Then, slowly let these sounds slowly fade away and bring back your awareness to your thoughts.

45

You don't have to try and control your thoughts. You just have to let them be, just like what you did with the sounds. Whatever thoughts come across your mind, try to see if you can picture them out as mental events in your mind, and let them stay there for a while.

You might also notice some emotions slowly emerging. Don't try to push them away. Instead, welcome them, no matter what they are. Rest in awareness. If your mind gets distracted, always remember that you can get back to the breath to ground you to the present moment.

For the last moments of this practice, bring back your focus to your breathing. Remember how your breathing can help take you back to the present when your mind starts to wander. It helps you be in a place where you can achieve peace and stillness.

The Intensely Frustrating Line Meditation

Waiting in line in the supermarket can be a great time to meditate. While lining, try to be more aware of your thoughts and reactions when something is trying to hold up your progress. Maybe, are you thinking of switching to a different line? Use this moment to be aware of what is going through your mind, what sensations are in your body, and what reactions you are aware of.

If you start to feel impatient because things are moving slower than what you expected, then you are probably in the Doing mode and in autopilot. Feeling that is okay, and is not wrong.

However, mindfulness will help you by differentiating the primary and secondary types of suffering. The primary suffering is what initially stresses you out, such as waiting in a long line. Secondary suffering is what you feel after experiencing the primary suffering, such as frustration, impatience, anger, and other thoughts that could arise along with these emotions.

Now, try to see if you can allow the feelings of frustration and anger to be present without trying to get rid of it. Stand tall, breathe, and be in the moment. You might still feel frustrated and impatient while waiting in line, but if you are aware of them, it is less likely that they would go out of your control.

Habit Releaser: A Visit to the Movies

Invite a family or friend to go out with you to watch a movie. Instead of planning ahead what film to watch, choose what movie you want to see when you get there. Arrange a time that you want to watch it, and then go to the movies and pick a film only when you're there. Many unexpected moments in life can make people their happiest. Movies can be a perfect practice for this.

A lot of people only go to watch a movie when they have a specific film they want to watch. However, if you try and take some time to go out to the movies spontaneously with no plans of what to see, you will find a totally different experience. You could end up watching a film that you never knew you would like. By doing this, you open your awareness of things and get to know yourself even more.

Before you head on to the movies, notice your thoughts before you left. You may think that you don't have the time to watch any film, or that you might not enjoy anything. These are what you call Practice Interfering Thoughts (PITs), and these thoughts will try to put down your enthusiasm to do things. These thoughts are pitfalls that people encounter every day, discouraging them to do something that could have been beneficial and nourishing for their lives. When you get to the movies, let go of any of these thoughts and just be in the moment, watching the film.

Chapter 9: Mindfulness Week Five: Turning Toward Difficulties

Whenever people are placed in a difficult situation, whether it's the feeling of sadness, losing a loved one, or being stressed, the natural response for many is to push these thoughts away. This can be done by ignoring these thoughts or by burying them under an endless pile of distractions. Mindfulness does not teach you detachment, it teaches you acceptance.

However, what is acceptance? To accept means to receive something, which could also mean to grasp or to understand. Acceptance enables the mind to grasp the truth, and to understand deeply how things truly are. Acceptance is pausing, in order to give time to let things be, to allow things to be as they are, and to see clearly. Acceptance gives you time to make better reactions to situations. It allows you to be aware of any struggles, difficulties, and pain, and to give wiser and more skillful responses. It helps you discover that there are times when the best way to respond is by doing nothing at all. Mindfulness gives you can chance to make choices.

Exploring Difficulty Meditation

Sit down in an upright posture for a few minutes. Bring your awareness into the sensations of your breath, and then take in the entire body. Next, start bringing your focus to the sounds and thoughts.

If you start to notice your attention slowly drifting into negative thoughts or emotions, acknowledge them. Now, with gentle control, bring your mind back to focusing on your breath, or your body or whatever it is that you wanted to focus on.

If you want a little challenge, instead of trying to bring the mind back from some thoughts and feelings, try to allow your thoughts and feelings to enter the mind and stay there. Then, direct your attention to your body, and notice any regions of your body that are feeling any pain or tension – physical sensations that arise along with thoughts or emotions. Now that you are aware of such sensations, consciously move your attention to the part of your body where you find the sensations strongest. Remember that the intention is not to change any sensations, but to be aware of them and to explore them. Tell yourself that it is okay to feel any of these emotions, and that it is okay to allow yourself to welcome it. Direct your full attention into these sensations, allowing your breath to flow through them. You don't have to like any of these feelings, it is natural not to want any of them. However, you must let go of any tendency to tense up and brace against any of your difficult thoughts.

If the sensations are slowly fading away, decide if you want to get back to focusing on your breath, or if you want to bring up a new difficulty in mind. If no strong physical sensations arise, then simply breathe in and out of any sensations that you feel in your body, even though they do not link to any particular feeling or emotion. To end this practice, return your attention to your breath, and its sensations as it moves along your body.

Habit Releaser: Sow Some Seeds (Or Look After a Plant)

Nurturing a plant, or sowing some seeds, are among those very simple things in life that can have a surprisingly big benefit. It might even save your life. In the late 1970s, Harvard University psychologist Ellen Langer and her team conducted a now classic series of experiments in which they tasked several elderly people in a care home to look after their own plant. They were told it was their responsibility to water it and make sure it received enough food and light. At the same time, another group of elderly people had a plant placed in their room, but were told "not to worry about it."

The nurses would look after it for them. The researchers then measured the levels of happiness in the two groups of people and found, and surprisingly, those who were asked actively to look after a plant were noticeably happier and healthier. They lived longer too. Just the act of caring for another living thing had markedly improved their life. So this week, why not sow some seeds, or buy, or borrow a plant from a friend?

Chapter 10: Mindfulness Week Six: Trapped in the Past or Living in the Present?

Do you treat yourself with kindness? Alternatively, do you often judge yourself? One of the most essential steps to finding peace is to learn how to treat yourself kindly.

Many people who enter mindfulness classes can't seem to be able to discover the message of kindness for themselves. They often see mediation as a kind of activity, another thing they should do.

In order to allow inner peace to radiate in you and to sustain this light, you must perceive the world through the lens of kindness and compassion. To do this, you must embrace who you are and treat yourself with love, honor, and respect.

The last mediation that you will be introduced to is the befriending meditation. This will teach you to be kind to yourself first, before you can bring kindness to others.

The Befriending Meditation

Spend a few minutes to allow yourself to settle in a comfortable place alone. Stay there and relax for a while. Stay in a posture that makes you feel dignified and awake. If you are sitting down, sit straight – shoulders wide, chest open, spine long.

Start to bring your attention to your breath, and then expand this attention to the entire body for a few minutes. When your mind starts to wander, be aware of where it went. Remember that you now know two ways to deal with this – either to bring back your awareness to whatever you intend to focus on, or to bring your attention to your body and focus on the sensations that you are experiencing. You can use any of the meditations in the previous chapters to help you prepare for this last one.

When you have settled and are ready, let any – or all – of these phrases to enter your mind. You can alter the words so they connect to you more and become your gateway to self-acceptance and friendliness.

> *May I be free from suffering.*

> *May I be as happy and healthy as it is possible for me to be.*

> *May I have ease of being.*

Pause and listen. Notice your physical sensations, and try to explore them without judging yourself. Stay at this moment for a while, and when you're ready, think of a loved one whom you want to wish well and say the same phrases.

> *May he (she/they) be free from suffering.*
>
> *May he (she/they) be as happy and healthy as it is possible for them to be.*
>
> *May he (she/they) have ease of being.*

Next, think of a stranger. This could be someone that you recognize, but don't know personally, such as a person in the bus or street. Recognize that even if you do not know them, they have their own dreams and fears. Keep them in your mind and heart, and wish them well. Say the same phrases above.

Now, wish peace to someone whom you've had some difficulties with. With proper intentions, and with all your mind and heart, say the phrases and wish them well.

Finally, extend these wishes to everyone – your family, your loved ones, other strangers, and other people whom you've had difficulties with. The importance here is to send intentionally love and friendship to everyone.

To finish this practice, sit with full awareness of the present. Whatever you feel by doing this practice, acknowledge your strength for being able to spend time to nourish yourself.

Habit Releaser

For this week, you will have two habit releasers to choose from, or you can also do both.

1. Reclaiming your life

Look back into a time when your life was less stressful and busy. Try to recall some activities that you did. This could be things you did alone, like reading or listening to music, or with your family and friends, such as playing video games or going out to the movies.

Choose one activity and try to do it once this week. The intention of this practice is to bring you back to a part of your life that you may have forgotten. This is a part of you that you thought you have already lost and could never get back to. This week, don't try to wait until you feel that you want to do it. Plan an activity and do it during the planned day and time, and see what happens. Notice how you feel, being able to do the things you thought you could never do again.

2. Do a good-natured deed for someone else

Carry out a random act of kindness to anyone. This could be a colleague, a neighbor, or a random stranger. You don't have to do something grand. Even a simple tidying of your workmate's desk could help bring some light into their day. In addition, you don't have to let them know that you did it. Just do it as an act of kindness, and notice how you feel. See how it could affect your body and your entire day.

Chapter 11: Mindfulness Week Seven: When Did You Stop Dancing?

Being aware of how much you spent being devoted to emotionally and physically draining activities is good, but it is also equally important to take action. You could spend less time doing these depleting activities. If you can't, then try to spare a little more time to do nourishing practices. Week seven is intended to help you take action and establish a balance between things that drain you and those that nourish you.

Step One: Rebalancing Your Daily Life

Take some time to reflect on how you can create a balance between your nourishing and draining activities. It is important to know that there are some aspects in your life that you cannot immediately change. For example, you might encounter some difficulties in your job, but you also cannot afford to quit it. If you encounter a lot of situations like this, then you have two choices.

The first option is for you to try your best to devote more time doing nourishing activities and to decrease time doing things that deplete you.

For the second option, you can try to deal with depleting activities differently. Try to become more present when you are doing them, even if they can be really unpleasant or boring. Try to be more mindful instead of thinking negatively towards doing these activities. By being in the present and being more mindful, you can learn to be more accepting of the good and bad things that happened during your day. You will also learn to be happier and more fulfilled.

Step Two: Breathing Space Plus Taking Further Action

The breathing space is not just a way for you to reconnect to your awareness. It could also serve as a powerful tool to help you take further action.

After doing all the meditation practices, you may have already learned that the way you perceive the world has slowly changed to become clearer and more anchored in reality. After you have grounded yourself to reality through your breathing exercises and other meditation practices, you are now ready to take on the world with skillful action. When you start to feel stressed, always remember to take a deep breath – a breathing space – before you consider how you must act.

For this week, try to focus on doing something not because you feel like doing it. Do it because you just have to do it. An example would be the habit releaser that asked you to go out to the movies. You may think that you might not like to go, but you just had to do it. Surprisingly, you enjoyed it.

Whenever you start to feel unhappy, tired, or stressed, waiting for that motivation to come in might not be the best idea. Sometimes, you have to act first before you can feel motivated. *When mood is low, motivation follows action, rather than the other way around. When you put the action first, motivation follows.*

Chapter 12: Mindfulness Week Eight: Your Wild and Precious Life

Most people today don't have time to acknowledge their little accomplishments in life. People would usually rush to finish a task, and when they do, they immediately start another one without taking a break. For many people, it is impossible to find even a short gap in between every task to realize that they just completed something. What happens is the opposite: it's just people thinking that they never achieved anything the entire day.

Learning to cultivate a sense of completeness in your life can help you appreciate your tiny achievements. This will make it easier for you to cope with your thoughts that would tell you that you have not fulfilled anything and that you are not yet happy. Establishing a sense of completeness will make you feel whole, no matter where you are in life.

Finding Peace in a Frantic World

Finding peace in a frantic world can be difficult, but not impossible. You can feel extremely overwhelmed with stress and anxiety and be limited by a negative mindset. These are all signs that you might be doing something wrong in your life, and that you must start paying more attention.

Once you have learned this, you will start to open the doors to a new approach to life – a more encouraging and positive approach. You will realize that you have to live each day in the present, that you must fully be in the here and the now. Many people unknowingly and unintentionally tend to postpone their lives. They think about catching up with their sleep in the weekend, or getting some rest and relaxation when the summer comes. However, the thing is, you lose a lot of moments in your life if you let this happen. Now is the only moment that you really have, and this is what mindfulness teaches. It tells you to be fully aware of the life that you currently have, instead of constantly living in a world of wishes and misinterpretation.

For week eight, you are encouraged to live the rest of your life. This time, go through each day with full awareness of everything that you do. Your task now is to incorporate all the practices that you learned into your life by creating a routine that would work for you in the long run.

Conclusion

Mindfulness is not an alternative to psychotherapy; it is a way of self-help. Mindfulness is not a special technique to help you understand the past or correct the present. It does not impose nor try to heal. Instead, it helps you become aware of your difficulties so that you learn for yourself how you must deal with them. It helps you reveal the underlying forces that drives these difficulties.

Mindfulness touches the hidden themes in your life, and when these are brought into awareness, you will start to feel the negativity slowly fading away. The endless struggles, being lost in your head, getting controlled by the autopilot, getting swallowed by the negativity – these are all representations of the Doing mode doing the best that it can to remedy certain situations. By practicing mindfulness, you learn to let go of viewing these as enemies that you must get rid of. You learn that these will all eventually go away as you start to establish a sense of awareness within yourself and with the world.

Final Thoughts

Hey! Did you enjoy this book? We sincerely hope you thoroughly enjoyed this short read and have gotten immensely valuable insights that will help you in any areas of your life.

Would it be too greedy if we ask for a review from you?

It takes 1 minute to leave 1 review to possibly influence 1 more person's decision to read just 1 book which may change their 1 life. Your 1 minute matters and we value it and thank you so much for giving us your 1 minute. If it sucks, just say it sucks. Period.

FREE BONUS

P.S. Is it okay if we overdeliver?

Here at Abbey Beathan Publishing, we believe in overdelivering way beyond our reader's expectations. Is it okay if we overdeliver?

Here's the deal, we're going to give you an extremely valuable cheatsheet of "Accelerated Learning". We've partnered up with Ikigai Publishing to present to you the exclusive bonus of "Accelerated Learning Cheatsheet"

What's the catch? We need to trust you… You see, we want to overdeliver and in order for us to do that, we've to trust our reader to keep this bonus a secret to themselves. Why? Because we don't want people to be getting our exclusive accelerated learning cheatsheet without even buying our books itself. Unethical, right?

Ok. Are you ready?

Simply Visit this link: http://bit.ly/acceleratedcheatsheet

We hope you'll enjoy our free bonuses as much as we've enjoyed preparing it for you!

Free Bonus #2: Free Book Preview of Summary: Jab, Jab, Jab, Right Hook

The Book at a Glance

Gary Vaynerchuk likens doing business to boxing. The way a boxing match goes is closely similar to how businesses and consumers interact with each other. In the modern setting, of which social media marketing is an essential part, businesses jab their consumers by providing content that can entertain and inform. Depending on how the consumers respond, the business can then proceed to jab some more or go for a right hook, which is equated to the sale or closing of the deal. This engagement is what Gary believes to be the driving force between business-consumer interaction online and offline.

In this book, Gary intends to educate businesses and marketers, especially those with small businesses, in the way of social media marketing. With his expertise and experience from his own success and his clients' from VaynerMedia, he hopes to teach the reader how to succeed in getting their brand known by their target audience. In doing so, the reader will hopefully be able to capitalize and create results from effective offers and promotions done on social media platforms.

The first few chapters of this book delve on the current set-up of the world regarding use of mobile devices and social media networks. The progress of this evolution in media has happened in the same way in previous forms, particularly in print, radio, and television. He also iterates how the modern story-telling process works in marketing and how it was shaped to its current form by social media. Then, he enumerates valuable pointers on how to create valuable content that will be effective jabs to make your audience relate with your brand.

In the next part, he builds upon the characteristics of good content to provide insight on current best practices and effective marketing strategies on the most used social media platforms. Facebook, Twitter, Pinterest, Instagram, and Tumblr are tackled individually. For each of these platforms, the right kind of content is explained and some tips are given on how to create effective content native to the platform. He also explores the opportunities from some of the emerging social media networks.

Transitioning from the different social media platforms, he explains the importance of effort to achieve success in any area of life. He says that it is true that small businesses have a great disadvantage when it comes to resources. This greatly affects their capability to match the marketing efforts of bigger businesses. However, the disadvantage of being a small organization is an advantage in of itself as it enables such businesses to respond at a faster rate to their audience's needs, interests, and preferences. He reiterates that, depending on the quality of effort exerted, advantages such as capital, budget, and human resource can be overcome.

In the last part, he states that the requirements for success in the modern day are a lot more different than those in the past. This is mostly due to the technological and socio-cultural changes brought on by various modern advancements. More changes will occur and things will get more difficult. Nevertheless, in the scheme of things, this shouldn't be the problem if your mindset is that of constant learning and development to achieve and maintain the leading position. Having this mindset will equip you to always fight for that position and, in the process, you will constantly grow as a professional.

Introduction: Weigh in

Business, like boxing, has an aggressive, competitive, and fast-paced feel to it. This is no different in the world of social media marketing. Companies create big campaigns or promotions to create results that will give them advantage over their competition. Like the right hooks in boxing, they know that these events deliver sales and the return of investment for their business.

In the current setting, marketers create campaigns one after the other but they still fail in creating the results they are after. This failure is borne out of the assumption that, with a well-executed right hook, one can lessen or forego creating relationships with their customers. It would have worked in the age of television and digital media; however, social media has changed the dynamics of business-customer interaction.

Frequent and numerous promotional offers just do not work as much anymore as today's business; like boxing, it does not consist only of right hooks. Yes, often, only the right hook is seen as the punch that won the match. However, without the boxer (the business) delivering jabs (customer engagement), the delivery of the "right hook" would surely miss. Either the recipient of such promotions would ignore it or it will have no audience at all as it did not provide the requisite jabs for customer engagement.

The inspiration for this book came from the realization that Gary's success for Wine Library TV was a result of authentic and genuine content suited for YouTube. The author emphasized in his previous book, *The Thank You Economy*, and in his various speaking engagements that social media marketing should be done with the long-term in mind. There should be genuine and solid customer engagement as this will create active and real relationships with one's customers. However, as Gary realized, sales and return on investment cannot be achieved by only using customer engagement. There should be well-executed "right hooks", or campaigns and sales as well, to create the revenue that will spell success for the business.

In his first book, *Crush It!*, Gary taught the readers how to create great content and how to utilize content for the different platforms available at that time. Nevertheless, the changes in existing platforms and development of new ones have brought about the need to change past approaches to deliver successful right hooks in the current setting. With this book, all the knowledge from the first two books will be updated and combined to illustrate how to apply it in the current social media and digital environment.

Regardless of the type of company or organization you're in, your task is to tell the story of your organization, company, or brand to your customer. Especially now that what was done in print, radio, and television has a smaller audience as to what it used to before, and direct e-mails and banner ads are not as effective as before. The only option for the most effective marketing is through social media as this is where people spend most of their time now.

This book will set you up in how to tell your story on the most important social media platforms of the time. The storytelling formula will be taught to you so that your story will be effective delivering your message to your customers. An examination of some of the good, bad, and ugly stories done by different companies will be done to illustrate the common pitfalls in social media marketing. Once you've learn all this book can teach, you will be able to adapt to any new platforms in the future.

Jab, Jab, Jab, Right Hook is considered to be the last book in Gary Vaynerchuk's trilogy on the evolution of social media and of his career as a marketer and businessman. Although the world and the available platforms change, the secret to creating results remains the same. To attain brand awareness and profit through social media marketing, it requires the classic and everlasting values of hard work, passion, constant engagement, sincerity, long-term commitment, and clever and strategic storytelling.

SUMMARY:

No-drama Discipline

THE WHOLE-BRAIN WAY TO CALM THE
CHAOS AND NURTURE YOUR CHILD'S
DEVELOPING MIND

ABBEY BEATHAN

Legal & Disclaimer

The information contained in this book is not designed to replace or take the place of any form of medicine or professional medical advice. The information in this book has been provided for educational and entertainment purposes only.

The information contained in this book has been compiled from sources deemed reliable, and it is accurate to the best of the Author's knowledge; however, the Author cannot guarantee its accuracy and validity and cannot be held liable for any errors or omissions. Changes are periodically made to this book. You must consult your doctor or get professional medical advice before using any of the suggested remedies, techniques, or information in this book. Images used in this book are not the same as of that of the actual book. This is a totally separate and different entity from that of the original book titled: "No Drama Discipline: The Whole-Brain Way To Calm The Chaos And Nurture Your Child's Developing Mind"

Upon using the information contained in this book, you agree to hold harmless the Author from and against any damages, costs, and expenses, including any legal fees potentially resulting from the application of any of the information provided by this guide. This disclaimer applies to any damages or injury caused by the use and application, whether directly or indirectly, of any advice or information presented, whether for breach of contract, tort, negligence, personal injury, criminal intent, or under any other cause of action.

You agree to accept all risks of using the information presented inside this book. You need to consult a professional medical practitioner in order to ensure you are both able and healthy enough to participate in this program.

Table of Contents

The Book at a Glance

If you are parent, you are very much familiar with this scenario: your kid misbehaves, it triggers your anger, you spank or yell at them, and the kid resorts to wailing. Too much drama, isn't it? This book will help will you deal with that kind of difficult moment. It will tackle the essential goals of discipline – the short-term aspect of immediate cooperation and the long-term goal of learning life skills. Furthermore, it will tackle ways to come up with a firm No-Drama, Whole-Brain disciplinary philosophy.

In Chapter 1, we will discuss what it really means to discipline a child and tackle different No-Drama discipline strategies. Chapter 2 will give a detailed discussion on the relationship of a child's developing brain and discipline. Chapter 3 will focus on the essence of showing love and connection to children despite the firm disciplinary approach. In relation to that, Chapter 4 will discuss effective strategies on creating connection with our kids to keep them calmer so they may really absorb everything we teach them; thus, helping them develop better decision-making skills.

After connecting, it is now time to redirect. With this, Chapter 5 will discuss the principle of discipline as a manner of teaching. Lastly, Chapter 6 will discuss different approaches to redirection in order to achieve the dual goal of discipline – encouraging immediate cooperation and teaching kids life-long internal skills.

This book aims to redefine discipline from most people's wrong conclusion that it is a form a punishment or control. There are effective ways to make discipline less of a drama and more of a connection between you and your child. Surprisingly, this book will give you the realization that disciplining moments should not be full of aggression and heartaches; rather, it can actually be used to build skills that would help your child as they grow into adulthood.

Before You Read This Book

A Question

Ask yourself if you are open to learning a different approach to discipline – a kind of approach that encourages immediate cooperation from your child right at that moment, and a long-term goal of molding them into individuals who are kind, successful, healthy and of course well-disciplined?

If you answered yes, this is exactly the book that you need.

INTRODUCTION

More often than not, it is hard to discipline our kids. They do something unruly, we get frustrated and resort to lecture or spanking. Then, they would get upset at us and begin shedding tears. It gets really frustrating when dealing with all the chaos and drama and we sometimes ask ourselves if there really is a calmer way of disciplining our kids.

To define the word discipline, we can look back to its origin. It came from the Latin word *disciplina* which means teaching, giving instruction and learning. Therefore, discipline, contrary to what most parents think, is not about punishing or controlling. Rather, it is about treating your child as a student and letting him learn (be it through instructions or through reflecting in his own behavior).

There are two goals of an effective discipline – first, to have our child's cooperation right at that moment and second, to build internal life-long skills that would help lessen the disciplining acts in the future. If a child misbehaves in a restaurant by consistently running around and disturbing other guests, we would want to make her stop right at that moment. But our second goal must be to make her develop self-control and stick the lesson in her mind so that when she comes back to the restaurant next time, she wouldn't repeat the same unruly behavior.

When we discipline our kids, remember that it must revolve around our relationship and emotional connection with them. We want to discipline our child in a way that they would feel our nurturing love and support. In fact, every time our children misbehave is the moment that they badly need to feel our connection. Simply put, firm disciplinary philosophies must work in balanced with empathic connection. As a result, it will help our children be better persons as they grow into adulthood. We'd be able to give them the opportunities to focus more on their brain's responsive rather than reactive state, hence, creating more venues of developing internal and life-long skills.

Chapter 1

It is common to hear parents complain their frustrations on disciplining their child. There are parents who know in their hearts that spanking and time-outs wouldn't do good but still can't think of better ways than that, while there are others who get confused between being calm and being too strict, and there are others who still battle daily with their four-year-old and doesn't seem to win every time their kid resorts to drama and tears.

In order to come up with a firm philosophy and principle-driven discipline approach, let us, first, rethink what discipline is. To break it all to you, discipline is not simply imposing time-outs and battling over dramatic arguments, rather, discipline is guided by a set of parenting philosophies.

Discipline must have a dual goal – the short-term and the long-term. First, it must encourage good external behavior and second, it must shape the brain's internal structure for building better behavior, life skills and relationship skills. This kind of approach on discipline requires parents to have a clear set of parenting responses and firm set of intentions.

However, instead of being responsive and intentional, parents often resort to simply being reactive. Imagine your kid playing with her set of dolls while you are busy drowning yourself in take-home office works. Suddenly, your kid throws her doll at you, hitting you in the face. Most parents would be reactive in this situation by letting their anger control them, allowing them to grab the kid in her puny arm, clench their fist so the grip becomes tighter and with big eyes and clenched teeth, lecture the kid on why throwing something at someone and hitting them is bad.

Of course, it is just normal for us to resort in a reactive way during a heated and raging moment of anger. Worse, it is more difficult not to react with anger especially if we, as parents, are too tired, stressed or haven't had a good sleep last night.

However, instead of being reactive, there is a better way of responding to our kid, something that would help us achieve the short-term goal of reducing such unlikely behavior and the long-term goal of building up life skills.

The Three Questions to a No-Drama Discipline

Let us have a piece-by-piece look into the situation above. Why? Why did my kid react that way? If we would let our anger be peppered with merely assumptions, perhaps our answer to this would simply be "Because she is having tantrums!" If we would just curiously look into our children's behavior, we would get a better understanding on what drove them to push such act. It would allow us to see that our child simply attempted at doing something but just didn't know how to handle it right. As a bonus, this would allow us to have a more personal relationship with our kid by acting compassionately. Why did your kid hit you with the doll? You were too busy on your paper work that you didn't notice she was struggling to put on her doll's clothes. Upon looking closely, that's the only time you would realize that she wanted your attention and help in putting on her doll's clothes. Since she was struggling to do the right thing, her brain was ignited with frustration, thus, throwing the doll at you.

What? What do I want to teach my kid right now? The end goal of discipline is to always teach valuable life lessons that would benefit the kid in the long-term. You may want her to learn that there are better ways of getting your attention and violence is not acceptable.

How? How can I teach this lesson? Reactive parents often resort to time-outs. This may or may not give your kid the lesson about not resorting to violence but the better way to do it is by connecting with her. You may hug her closer to you to help her calm the anger and frustrations down. This way, she would know that she has your attention now. As she becomes calmer, talk with her and discuss better ways of getting your attention like approaching you with words instead. Just remember to do this at a moment when you are both in a receptive, and not reactive, state of mind.

When we discipline on reactive mode, we often just see things in our own perspective. We tend to forget to assess what our child really needed at that moment. We tend to just assume We tend to forget that they are just children whose brains are not yet fully developed. Example, when a child whose been sitting for about half an hour begins to wail, we tend to assume that giving him something to distract his wails would be the answer. When in fact, what we must do is think of what he needs at the moment – maybe he needs to get up and stretch his legs. Sometimes, it frustrates us because we expect them to tell us exactly what they need but they simply can't because of their developmental capacity.

Therefore, it is important to choose moment-by-moment decisions and not just a one-size-fits-all expectation that we apply to every circumstances. It is important to consider a child's age or developmental stage, his emotional capacity, the environment, etc. Even the most popular one-size-fits-all disciplinary technique which is spanking and time-out can't be reliable.

Spanking and Time-Outs

There are different kinds of parents just as there are different kinds of children. Based on most literature, spanking can only make teaching less effective. It is often associated with negative outcomes even when parents still remain loving and nurturing after spanking their child. Even the non-physical violence such as threatening, humiliating, and screaming at them can wound a child's mind. It is therefore encouraged that parents do not resort to any form of disciplinary technique that creates fear, pain, terror and aggressiveness. First, these are counterproductive approaches. The technique would only make the "goal" ineffective because instead of reflecting at his own behavior, the child's attention would only be directed to how mean or terrifying his parent is. Second, they only bring negative neurological and physiological effects. Spanking would only cause disorganized attachment in a child's brain. The basic human instinct is to cling towards the parent for safety and protection. However, it is a human instinct, too to escape from someone who inflicts pain and terror. If the parent is also the cause of pain and terror, the child's brain would be in a disorganized state and repeated moments of these can bring long-lasting negative impacts on a child's brain like the death of brain cells. Third, instead of engaging the child's receptive brains, spanking will only trigger the reactive state that prevents them from making healthy decisions.

There are parents who think that time-outs are better options than spanking. However, time-outs would neither help achieve the dual goals of No-Drama Discipline. First, instead of allowing the child to reflect on his behavior, time-outs would only give them time to reflect on their parent's behavior – like assuming how mean they are for giving them such disciplinary action. Second, it gives them the psychological feeling of abandonment. When a child wails because she got frustrated over her spilled milk, time-out would only aggravate her disappointment. Instead, think of what she needs at the moment – maybe she needs a reassurance that there is still milk available for her so she won't get hungry again. Discipline is not about letting a child pay for her mistake, rather, it is about letting her self-regulate her emotional overload.

No-Drama discipline would build-up the skills and connections in the brains that allow the child to make thoughtful decisions and take better control of their emotions. Therefore, as they go along, disciplinary actions would be needed less each time. As parents, you may ask yourself questions that would help in creating a disciplinary philosophy. You may assess what really is your disciplinary technique and how do you and your child feels about it. You may reflect if this technique is effective and how does it affect your relationship with your child.

It is important to know what you really want for your kids. You cannot always do it perfectly every time but if you would take effort on developing self-control when your kids behave badly; you can achieve the dual goal of discipline. Through this, you can also lessen the times of over-reacting and instead, behave with a responsive and intentional sense. A child's brain changes its structure through new experiences and a responsive and intentional approach is what they need for the health of their developing brains.

Chapter 2

Not only is the human brain changing, it is also changeable and complex – it allows us to respond to any situation we are in. It can also affect how we, as parents, take control and administer disciplinary decisions. However, remember that our children's state of brain development should also be considered in teaching them discipline. There are three important discoveries about the human brain that will be discussed in this chapter and we will brand them as the 3C's.

The Brain is Changing, Changeable and Complex

The anatomy of a child's brain is comparable to a building that is still under construction with a lower and upper level.

The lower level is primitive and controls fundamental functions like sleep cycle, breathing and digestion, and most importantly, strong human emotions and instinct.

The upper level which controls more complex thinking only starts to develop during the early stages of infancy and childhood. It is the one responsible for sophisticated thinking including relationship and emotional skills, regulation of emotions, sound decision-making and morality. Sounds beautiful, right? These are exactly what we want our children to achieve until they grow older. However, they require a fully functional upper brain that takes a long time to develop. But it doesn't mean that they are of no use during the childhood years. It just means that the basic upper brain structure that was built during the early stages of life will simply be changing during adulthood.

Now, it is clearer to see that no matter how much we try, our kids won't behave like an adult simply because that's how their brains are being constructed. It would even be unfair to our children if we expect them to always handle themselves well and take control of their emotions at all times. One mistake we often do is looking at how our children react based on our own set of "adult" and fully-developed mind, when in fact, we need to consider their own point of view and what they are only capable of during their developmental stage. We need to adjust our expectations especially because a child's capacity to react well depends on specific context like if she is tired or sleepy or hungry. Example, a sleepy child would likely wail during a supposed nap time as compared to a well-rested one. The wailing is simply an instinctual way of communicating how she feels at that time.

When we understand that their brains are changing, it allows us to listen closely to our kids with more empathy and understanding. It allows us to not only react on the external factors but also see what they are seeing in their own developing minds.

The difference between the brain as changing and being changeable is that the former refers to it as something that develops over time, while the latter means it is moldable. It can be intentionally and/or unintentionally changed through the experiences we undergo.

All of these experiences take place in the brain's neurons and synapses. A Canadian neuropsychologist named Donald Hebb has come up with the term, "Hebb's Axiom"; which simply means that the neurons in our brains fire up and form a certain network every time we experience something. When these experiences are repeated over and over again, this network of neurons receives stronger and deeper connections. Example, someone who repeatedly enrolls in cooking classes during his younger years will most likely become a good chef when he grows up.

Therefore, if it has already been scientifically proven that experience changes the physical formation of a brain; then, as parents we need to be extra careful with what we let our children experience. Everything they experience with all their senses will have an impact on how they view and interact with their environment and the world. Hence, we may want to review the kind of games they play, the movies they watch and the conversations that we let them hear.

However, as much as we want to, we still won't be able to control some negative experiences that would come along their way. But that doesn't mean that we cannot do something about it. What we can do is help our children walk through these challenging experiences and help them realize important lessons along the way.

As we said earlier, the brain has a lower and upper level. The upper brain is receptive and is responsible for calmer response and controlling the emotions while the lower brain is reactive and is responsible for anger and impulse.

Therefore, when your child throws tantrums at a public place; obviously, the lower brain is showing impulse. You can choose to yell and stop him immediately but that would only enrage him more. What if both of the child and the parent's lower brains are reactive; then, it is going to be a dramatic battle again.

The more effective way to handle such situation is take the brain's complexity into an advantage – engage the upper brain rather than enrage the lower brain. One trick to do so is acknowledging what she feels. When you both acknowledge what she feels, you are teaching her to calm that enraging feeling. It's a skill that can last a lifetime. Through repeated upper brain engagement, she'll become better at decision-making and reflecting her feelings first rather than reacting immediately.

Combining the three Brain C's and Applying Them

Sometimes no matter how much we try to apply the Brain C's, things will still not go perfectly. The kids won't still act and handle their emotions well. If that happens, the goal is to still remain empathic, connected and calm.

Kids won't still be able to act the way we want them all the time. However, the No-Drama discipline approach assures us of one thing – it builds relationship between parents and kids while it lessens the probability of heartache caused by yelling or spanking or not listening closely to them.

No-Drama discipline gives the child a feeling of acceptance and safety. If repeated effectively, it gives them the assurance of being loved – in good times and even when they mess up. They would feel that they are not required to be perfect all the time in order to gain our love, trust and acceptance. This gives them the freedom that would eventually lead to good decision-making skills. Unlike when a parent controls the child with fear and terror, it diminishes their freedom to move and decide for themselves. They will just always be afraid to make decisions and mistakes.

The no-drama discipline encourages the development of the upper brain by constantly giving the child the freedom to understand herself, understand her feelings, explore other options and make good decisions in every situation.

Aside from the benefits of being able to show our kids that they are loved, safe, and protected; the concept of the three Brain C's leads us to another important conclusion – No-Drama discipline builds the brain!

By teaching our children with the No-drama discipline approach, we are giving them the chance to strengthen the connection between the upper and lower brains. The way we communicate with them has an impact on how their brains develop and what kind of people they would be molded into. What we allow them to exercise in their upper brain will get stronger. Example, when we repeatedly give them the chance to decide rather than simply impose what to do, they develop into better decision-makers.

As parents, this is exactly what we want to achieve for our children – that they learn to make good choices from whatever situation they encounter and not to simply do what is imposed on them.

Setting Limits and Brain-Building

The autonomic nervous system has two parts – the sympathetic or accelerator (responsible for impulse) and the parasympathetic which is comparable to a break (responsible for regulating the impulse). So, when a child's accelerator is triggered but stopped immediately with a break (parental limitations), it creates a response which leads to a feeling of shame.

It is important that a parent sets limits for his/her child. When encountering limitations, a child's brain battles with the concept of good vs bad and/or acceptable vs not acceptable. This process helps her build her sense of conscience and helps regulate future behaviors.

One way parents set limitations is by saying an outright "NO" to their child even if it is unnecessary. However, an outright "No", especially if peppered with anger, only disregards the healthy feeling of shame or conscience within a child. This is called toxic shame, and repeated feeling of toxic shame can lead to a sense of defectiveness. This can affect how a child views herself and her relationship with others.

The most effective and best alternative to saying "no" is saying a "yes" but with condition. This gives the child her needed form without humiliating her.

If we look closely, children's misbehavior not only allows us to communicate with them; rather, they also communicate with us. When a child punched a friend for playing with his toys, he is communicating his need to build the virtue of sharing. Of course misbehavior and tantrums are unwanted responses from a child; however, it is important to look at these misbehaviors as opportunities for knowledge and growth. You have the opportunity to reconstruct them and look at them as chances to build the brains. As a result, it creates growth and meaningful experiences for a child.

Chapter 3

Connecting first is not only more warm and relational. It can be an effective way to achieve the dual goal of discipline – encouraging immediate cooperation and building the brains. Connecting first gives the child a reassurance that you could feel him, in turn; it calms all the emotional chaos. When the chaos turns into calm, the child gets a better opportunity to listen and better understand your teachings.

Connection is a powerful tool of disciplining when the child is in an emotional chaos. However, all of these can be avoided – yes, disciplining acts can be avoided – simply by being a proactive parent rather than reactive.

Be Proactive Rather than Reactive

To avoid having to discipline, look for warning signs of possible misbehavior and chaos. Example, when a child shows signs of being hot-tempered and impatient; be proactive and think of possible reasons for flashing those signs. Maybe you'd remember that your child acts that way when she fails to have a good night sleep. As a proactive parent, what you want to do is act immediately, like ask her to take a nap first in order to touch up the warning signs and prevent major misbehavior and disciplining acts later on. A good trick to being proactive is to HALT or ask yourself if your child is Hungry, Angry, Lonely or Tired.

Proactive parenting requires awareness on your part. If you could just effectively watch out for signs that your child is going to a direction that would require disciplinary actions later on, you'll end up avoiding them.

However, there are also moments when warning signs seem unavailable and misbehavior just happens in a snap. The best thing to do in such situation is not to react with anger but to connect first.

Connection is a powerful response to our kids' trouble and inability to control themselves. More than that, it offers the benefits which are short-term, long-term and relational.

The first benefit of connection is it moves our children from a state of reactivity to receptivity. When our children misbehave, it only means that they are having a hard time controlling and dealing with everything that's going on around them. Their minds are in a state of overwhelming storm and that's when they actually need us the most. When we begin connecting with them, their receptivity slowly overpowers the reactivity. After that, receptivity prepares them to effectively absorb what you want him to learn. Hence, it makes teaching more effective.

The second and long-term benefit of connection is brain-building. When we connect to our children by listening to them, feeling their feelings, and communicating our love for them despite of messing up; it impacts the way their brains develop. Connection and integration in a child-parent relationship give children a sense of empathy, compassion and other skills encouraged by the upper brain. In the long-term, it develops our children into people with decision-making skills, relationship skills and successful interaction with their environment.

Lastly, connection strengthens the bond and relationship between a parent and a child. When our kids act their ugliest behavior, it is so easy to forget connection and remember our anger. However, in any situation, especially in disciplinary ones, connection must always be a parent's first option. Not only it activates receptivity and build the brain, more importantly, it communicates how much a parent loves her child. The more empathy, support and security, and unconditional love we show them; the more the relationship would be valued and strengthen. This would give children the essence of unconditional love – that we still love them even if we are not happy with their actions and decisions.

Dealing with Tantrums

The truth about tantrums is that they shouldn't be ignored because ignoring them is equivalent to ignoring our children's suffering. Tantrums are external signs of internal distress. We know that tantrums are very distressing for the parent, too but dealing with it can be boiled down into asking yourself what kind of message you want to send to your child.

The most important message that you would want to send your child is that you are there with her, even in times of being upset. Of course, you want immediate ending to your child's tantrum. However, if a Whole-Brain approach is moving inside you, your bigger goal isn't stopping the tantrum immediately. Rather, the bigger goal would be to connect and make the child feel your presence. Again, this emotional responsiveness would benefit the child in the long run by helping her brain to develop better choices and control in the future.

With all the benefits of connection, including strengthening relationship by consistently listening to a child's feelings when they misbehave, some parents are worried that this might actually lead to spoiling. First off, spoiling is not about giving too much love or too much of yourself to your child. Letting your child know that she can count on you at all times doesn't make her spoiled. Rather, what spoils a child is when you create her a world of self-entitlement where she believes that she could get everything she wants.

Connection only means that we acknowledge our children and their needs but not giving them a sense that we could give whatever they want.

Spoiling occurs when children are given too much material things. It also happens when they get a sense that everyone will give into their whims. As a result, children grow up not knowing how to work hard for something and develop gratitude – life skills aimed by a No-drama discipline.

Connection, on the other hand, is not about giving in to our kids' whims or shielding them from challenging experiences but it is about just being there for them in times of any form of suffering. To do it effectively, we must know how to incorporate connecting with setting limits. Choose loving limits instead of limitless limits. The former is mainly about commanding and demanding a child to behave in a manner that we want. The latter is about setting limits while still connecting.

When we connect while setting limits, we allow our children to have a grasp of valuable lessons of respect and relational ability. Remember, the moment that our children are in their worst is the moment they badly need our presence and connection. In doing so, we have helped them be receptive, build their brains and strengthen their relationship with us.

Chapter 4

When our children need our presence during a difficult moment, it is important to exercise response flexibility in order to take the best action needed in that particular moment. Response flexibility is taking a pause first before responding to a scenario. It is basically the opposite of just diving into a one-size-fits-all respond to every situation. If we are flexible, we tend to reflect first with before taking any action. In this way, we are able to choose the best possible action to handle our kids during a difficult moment.

The first principle of a No-Drama discipline is to listen to the present and individual moment; not react from the frustrations of the past or the fear of future. Do not exaggerate the present situation but be aware of that individual moment you and your child are in.

It is not to say that it's just fine to ignore patterns of misbehavior. Of course denial is also a bad parenting style. Example, you convince yourself that it's understandable if your child raised his voice at you because that's what his friends are doing, too. Instead of being distracted by external voices, react on the situation based on present actual facts. Do not rely simply on your own assumptions. Connect to your child in a calmer way to be able to find out what he really needs at the moment.

In disciplining your child, take a pause first and feel what kind of internal voice you hear in your head. If it's a reactive voice that echoes subjectivity, anger, expectations and fears; take a moment first before responding to the situation. If you hear a voice that is receptive, loving, understanding and connecting; you may now respond to your kid's misbehavior. A flexible respond rather than a rigid reaction is a key to a No-Drama discipline.

Another connection principle to a No-Drama discipline is asking all the questions, especially the Why's, before responding. As a parent it is important that you disregard all the assumptions and emotions in your head to maintain objectivity. Do not react without even gathering enough data regarding the situation. Example, you yelled at your 9-year-old when you heard your toddler cry while they were both playing in the other room. You let anger echoed in your reactive voice when you assumed that it was the 9-year-old's fault simply because he has a record of making the toddler cry in the past. Suddenly, the toddler points to his knee and you guiltily realize that it wasn't the 9-year-old's fault. The toddler fell off the floor at his own movement.

Instead of making assumptions, blaming, and criticizing; ask the why's. Curiosity is one good foundation of an effective parenting discipline. Let curiosity overpower the anger and frustrations. Investigate your child's behavior and chase the why's like *"Why did she do that?" Why did this happen?"* As you investigate along the way and listen closely to your child, you will be surprised with an interesting, accurate, or maybe hilarious answer from her.

However, most children are not yet fully aware of their motivations and insights. They may not be able to answer your "why's". Therefore, it is important that you do not just ask the why's but chase the why's. The latter basically means becoming curious in your own mind and asking questions to yourself. This way, you'll be able to look further behind the child's behavior; to see the internal motives and not just the external actions.

Another connection principle is to listen closely to "how" you interact with your child. Unlike the previously mentioned strategies that focus on the child and parent's internal structure, this one is mainly about considering the manner of talking to your child.

What you say to your child is important so as how you say it. Encouraging cooperation will be more successful and satisfying when you consider your manner of interacting. This is because children cooperate more when they feel that they are connected. So, next time, do not say *"Finish your breakfast or else you'll be late for school!"* with clenched teeth and round, scary eyes. Instead, try to say the exact message with a calmer and softer voice, *"Finish your breakfast now. If you won't, we'll have a hard time making it to school on time. You don't want to be late, don't you?"* Discipline becomes more effective if the "how" is driven with calmness and connection.

The No-Drama Connection Cycle as Connection Strategies

Connecting with your child means making her feel that you understand her feelings. Connection follows a four-part process, though the cycle won't always be followed in the same exact order.

The first process of the Connection Cycle is communicating comfort. When your child is in an emotional chaos (that happens when she misbehaves), the first thing to do is help her calm down. Comforting words are helpful but what's really more powerful is nurturing nonverbally. One nonverbal response, and perhaps the most powerful of all, is touching your child. It is so powerful that when someone touches us in a loving way, it releases happy hormones and diminishes the stress hormones in our brains.

Sometimes we do not notice that even our posture, eye level and hands are nonverbal communication that sends a message to our children. In connecting with your child, allow your body posture to send a message of calmness and not threat. To do so, look at your child below her eye level. You may opt to kneel down or sit on a chair but just make sure that you are below her eye level. You may cross your arms or put them behind you, no matter which, make sure that your posture is relaxed and calm. Also, consider talking in a softer tone.

A combination of comforting words and relaxed posture is an effective way of connecting to your child. Nonverbal communication is powerful; it can send a message without you even talking.

The second process is validating your child and her feelings. Validation means letting your child know that you understand what she feels and you are attuned to her emotions. Do not impose how she must feel, like saying, *"Stop acting that way! You're not supposed to cry for not getting an A on your exam!"* Telling her what to feel will only invalidate her and make her feel unimportant, invisible, and worse; disconnected.

On the other hand, validating her feelings would bring connection between the two of you. It would let your child feel that you are still listening, feeling what she feels and staying with her even though you didn't like what she did. Remember, identifying the child's feeling is another key to connection.

The third process to the Connection Cycle is listening rather than talking. Most parents think that when their children do something wrong, the best way to teach discipline is lecture them. However, lecture and talking is the least effective respond during a child's emotional distress. Remember that a child's brain is still developing and changing and not yet fully functional. When a child is having a hard time dealing with her emotions, the upper brain which is responsible for logic and reason is quiet. Therefore, talking and lecture is useless. No wonder, some kids would reply *"Can you please stop talking right now, Mom?"* to a parent who is lecturing non-stop. Their brains cannot fully grasp your linguistic approach and would just worsen their distress.

The best thing to do, then, is listen and stop talking. Look for some clues in what she's saying in order to fully understand her. No matter how tempting it is to argue, just listen as your child expresses her feelings.

Lastly, as the fourth process in the Connection cycle, reflect on what you heard. When you've already communicated comfort, validated her feelings, and listened; it's now time to reflect to her everything that she's told you. It's a process of giving her a perspective of what she felt earlier. This is your chance to redirect her big emotions and convince her that it was just a momentary feeling and not a lifetime state. Example, tell her that you understand why she hated her brother for eating her cake in the fridge but let her remember how much she loves her brother and the happy bondings they had. In this way, you are giving her a perspective that the hate she felt was just there for a moment and not for a lifetime.

Others may say that the connection process is just a way of spoiling a child by giving too much attention. Again, too much attention will not spoil a child. In fact, attention is a vital need of any child anywhere. More so, what the connection cycle really does is it allows us to communicate comfort with our children, to let them know that we are just there with them and we see and feel them. This way, it strengthens a kind of connection that reflects love and support; and as a result, it will prepare them for an effective redirection.

Chapter 5

Redirection is what we do after connecting with our children in which we engage their upper brains. It is necessary to an effective disciplining. For a comprehensive explanation, discipline can be shortened into the phrase "1-2-3 discipline". It basically means one definition, two principles and three desired outcomes.

One Definition

There is a simple one word definition of discipline - teaching. It is not about giving punishment or consequences or fear and terror; it is about teaching. It is necessary to remember discipline this way so we'll not be off track on our way to achieving its vital goals.

When teaching, it is important to let your child exercise her upper brains. Instead of being reactive, allow the sensations (such as guilt) flow naturally in your child. Initiate conversation and allow her to express her feelings. This way, her sense of conscience will be awaken and this will help in molding her self-control and self-awareness.

Two Principles

There are two main principles that will guide you in redirecting, first is to wait until your child is ready, and second is to be consistent but not rigid.

A sweet spot is necessary to teaching and learning effectively. It refers to that moment when your child has fully transitioned from reactive to receptive state. The nervous system is the center of a child's learning; it should be ready in order to fully grasp whatever is being taught to her. It should neither be under aroused (like when a child is sleepy, tired or bored) nor over aroused (when the child is dealing with big emotions).

An effective redirection happens when you ask yourself first if your child is ready to listen and ready to learn. Alternatively, ask yourself if you are ready to teach, too. Simply put, both of you must be in a calm receptive state before teaching and learning discipline.

The second principle is to be consistent but not rigid. Consistency is like a basic rule in parenting however, there are some parents who go over the top in prioritizing consistency until it becomes rigid and unhealthy. Of course it is important to set out rules and be consistent at them but also remember that you must be flexible in responding to different situations.

Three outcomes

The first desired outcome of redirection is "insight". When you discipline through a No-Drama approach, you let your child reflect at her own actions and feelings by initiating conversations with her instead of jumping into sermons. As a result, she develops her sense of self-understanding and self-control.

Alternatively, "empathy" becomes the second outcome of redirection. After focusing on your child's personal insights, it's important to let her reflect at how her actions have affected others. Through this, she develops her sense of interconnection which is the basis of moral thinking and actions.

After focusing on a child's personal insights and reflecting at others' feelings through empathy, the third outcome of redirection is integration and repair. This is the part where you ask the child what she thinks she can do to repair the situation – is it saying sorry to her younger sister when she pulled her hair? In doing so, you are helping her activate and develop her upper brain which triggers responsible decision-making and morality.

The brain develops through different opportunities that life has in store for us. In parenting, we encounter different experiences, different opportunities and different struggles that require different actions. Again, they key is to respond flexibly based on that given moment. The 1-2-3 discipline is not a quick formula that you must memorize all the time or follow inflexibly. However, the 1-2-3 discipline will guide you better in disciplining your kids in a way that leads to better cooperation and better relationship between them and others. More importantly, better connection between the two of you.

Chapter 6

Keep calm and connect - that's the mantra you must follow when your child becomes hard to control and ballistic. When your child messes up, your goal is to redirect her into her upper brain. Before doing so, you must be in a receptive mode as well. It is important to take a pause, avoid reacting in a snap, keep your calm and ask yourself if you are ready.

Then, begin to connect with a loving and nurturing tone. Consider all the internal factors – how your child really feels and how she perceives what happened.

When it's time to discipline, the first step is to always keep calm then, connect. After which, you may turn to your redirecting strategies.

Dissecting the R-E-D-I-R-E-C-T-I-N-G Strategies

The specific redirection strategies we want to share with you can easily be remembered through an acronym R-E-D-I-R-E-C-T.

These are different strategies that you should keep and when circumstances requires, pick one that is suitable to that particular situation depending also on the child's temperament, stage and age, and your own specific parenting style.

R- educe Words

It is important to address the issue at hand but do it in a subtle talking. Do not overdue the lecture as it will only flood your child with more sensory output. When it happens, she is just going to shut you down in her brain because of her short attention span. Especially younger children or toddlers, their brains do not have yet the capacity to absorb long lectures.

Instead, to address a toddler behavior, follow these four steps: Connect and address the feelings behind the behavior, address the behavior, give alternatives, move on.

By moving on after addressing the behavior, you are giving the child a space and allowing her to not dwell on the negative behavior but instead go back to the right track.

E- mbrace Emotions

Embracing emotions means parent must help the child understand her feelings during redirection. It must be explained to the child that what she feels is neither right nor wrong and neither valid nor invalid - they just are; they are momentary feelings. However, addressing feelings doesn't mean accepting the bad behavior. So, you may send her a message like *"It's okay to feel angry at your little sister, you still love her, and your anger is just there for a moment. However, let's think of ways of feeling that anger other than pulling her hair."*

It's important to embrace your child's emotions because it would make her feel visible and respected. You want her to feel that you still acknowledge her emotions despite of you not liking what she did. In doing so, she'll be more open to learning discipline and whatever life skills you teach her.

D-escribe, Don't Preach

When a child misbehaves, the parent's first and immediate action might be to preach and sermon. However, a better approach would be to describe the behavior so she could see what exactly you want her to see. Instead of *"Stop playing with my makeup kit!"*, describe by saying, *"You're playing with my makeup again. That might be bad for your skin, honey"*.

Yes, you are teaching her the concept of good vs bad but remember that a short and clear message would be more powerful than a lengthy sermon. This goes back to the importance of "how". Also, describing the behavior gives the child enough opportunity to decide what she would do right at that moment, hence, exercising her upper brains. More importantly, describing initiates a conversation. This gives her a chance to explain, thus, creating more space of connection between the two of you.

117

I-nvolve Your Child in the Discipline Process

In disciplining their child, most parents think that it should always be a one-directional lecture approach where in the parent does all the talking and the child just keeps quiet and listens (explaining and butting in can even be considered as a bad behavior of talking back). However, the best approach to redirection is a two-directional approach that involves the child in the discipline process. If you involve the child in a collaborative dialogue, she'd feel more respected and open to whatever you are teaching her. Of course you still have the authority as a parent. A dialogue means the child's input is still being considered in the process but you still have the final say. When you involve the child in the discipline process, she'll be able to share her ideas on coming up with a resolution to fix the bad behavior, thus, she'll become a better problem solver.

R-eframe a No into a Conditional Yes

When a child makes a request, responding with an outright "no" peppered with a hard tone will only activate her reactive state. Instead of an outright "no", redirect the respond to a "yes with conditions". Do not say *"No! You can't have that ice cream!"* but say *"You want that ice cream? Okay, you can have it but you have to take your breakfast first"*. This way, she'd be able to see that despite the "no" at the moment she would still be given a "yes" before too long. More so, you are helping your child develop her sense of imagining future actions and her sense of possibilities. These are skills that can help her develop social and emotional intelligence.

E-mphasize the Positive

A common misconception about discipline is that it is nothing but negative when in fact, you shouldn't be focusing on negativities as a response to misbehavior. Looking only at the negative will just focus the process on the bad behavior that you don't want to be repeated. Instead, redirect the negative into positive. Example, do not say *"Stop scattering your toys on the floor!"* but say *"I would love it if you would begin tidying up your toys now"*. One trick to maintain consistency is to observe the kid until you catch her do something positive then, compliment her for doing so.

Embracing the positive will emphasize the good things that you want to be repeated. It gives your child a gentle encouragement to repeat them again in the future without even demanding or bribing with praises and rewards. It would make her feel that you notice and appreciate when she is making good decisions.

C-reatively Approach the Situation

This book has already mentioned that there is no one-size-fits-all approach to discipline. Every situation demands a different response. Thus, it is important that parents remain their response flexibility to be able to think of creative ways of handling a difficult moment.

Example, humor is a good tool in bursting your child's bubble of high emotions. Especially with toddlers, parents resort to showing off their comic skills like dancing silly or making funny faces to break the child's emotional distress. Then, change the dynamics of the situation so you can go back to the goal of discipline.

This kind of strategy is effective because the brain loves novelty. Showing off humor and novelty can easily get the brain's attention. This can easily diminish the sense of fear and threat in a child's brain, allowing her to open up to her environment and easily connect with others.

T-each Mindsight Tools

Mindsight is basically seeing our own minds (through personal insights), that of others (through empathy), and promoting integration from there. One tool you can use is the "hand model" approach. It is basically about reminding your child to open up the upstairs brain in order to calm down the overwhelming emotions in the downstairs brain. If repeated effectively, this gives the child the idea that she is the actor and director in that particular situation and she has the capabilities of deciding how the script would end. Example, when your child opens up her upper brains, instead of yelling at her younger sister for messing up her playdate with a friend, she would resort to calmly expressing her feelings of anger and call you to ask for help in carrying the little sister out of the room.

This way, you are helping your child develop skills of understanding others and what's happening around so she can take charge of her response by making intentional choices. It will help your child develop both the sensing and observing circuits. As a result, she will be able to see her environment differently by thinking about options other than what's making her upset at that moment. Mindsight tools give our children the opportunity to act upon their emotions rather than be controlled by them.

These mindsight tools, and other strategies discussed here, can be used every time you encounter a disciplining moment with your child. You can try incorporating these different strategies or pick one that best suits the current situation you and your child are experiencing. When you use these No-

121

Drama Whole-Brain strategies and approach, which can be boiled down into connecting and redirecting, you will be able to easily achieve the dual goals of discipline.

Conclusion

The No-Drama Whole-Brain approach makes discipline a lot loving, relational and connecting. It is a helpful tool for your child's personal development, brain development, life skills and relational development. It begins with acknowledging the basic needs of a child – attention, expression; and the need to be understood, supported, and loved. This kind of connection is essential in order to make teaching and discipline more welcomed and absorbed. It does not only help to stop the bad behavior immediately but it also helps in the development of life skills needed by a child to grow into a responsible, empathetic, and logical individual.

Every parent faces difficult situations with their child. You are going to face moments of anger and frustrations. In moments like that, you may want to remember these four messages of hope. These will help you find peace and solace during those difficult times.

First, sometimes there is no magic wand that would make bad situations disappear in a snap. Sometimes the best and only thing you could do is exert all the love and understanding that you could give to your child. There would be times when you know you've already done your best but your child still feels bad and upset. That's perfectly okay and it doesn't mean that you are a bad parent.

Second, it's okay to make mistakes as a parent and it doesn't make you a bad one either. There are times that you've done everything but still end up lowering down your levels and joining your kids' childishness. Don't feel heavy every time you mess up as a parent. Those may not be the best parenting techniques but as long as you show your kids that you know when and how to apologize for messing up, you are still giving them some lessons. You are giving them an idea that having self-compassion is necessary, too and they must be kind to themselves and to others. As a result, you are giving your child some lessons on love.

Third, conflict with our children is going to inevitably happen. Difficult moments would often lead to misunderstandings and arguments. However, you can still take hope by knowing that you still have plenty of chances to reconnect. You may even use these difficult moments to establish a stronger connection with your child by repairing the breach. Your kid will eventually soften and reconnecting will allow them to see your positive intentions.

Fourth, there are still plenty of chances to make a positive change and it's never too late for it. After reading all the chapters, you may have guiltily realized that you are neglecting your relationship with your child by making rigid disciplinary actions, or that you have missed a lot of past opportunities to build stronger connection. If that's the case, have hope by knowing that it's never too late. Remember that the brain is changing and changeable. If you feel like you've given your child negative impressions and experiences by your reactive responses in the past, then, you can still change her impressions. Of course you're not going to be perfect but you can decide whether or not to be a parent who is committed to her child's lifelong success, health and happiness.

A NOTE TO OUR CHILD'S CAREGIVERS

You are important to our children's lives and we share the same desire to mold them into individuals with good characters. We can work together by giving them effective discipline experiences as these eight principles guide us along the way.

1. Giving our children set of boundaries is essential in helping them become successful in their lives and in their relationship with others.

2. Discipline should never give them a sense of threat, fear and pain but a loving experience. The latter allows discipline to become more effective.

3. Discipline's goal is to teach and build our children's skills that will help them become good decision-makers.

4. It has been scientifically approved that acknowledging a child's emotion can make behavior-changing much easier.

5. To build trust and sense of safety, we need to show them that we are with them no matter what. During an emotional distress is when they need us the most.

6. The first step to teaching discipline is making sure the child has calmed down and is ready to listen. It is necessary to wait first until the child is ready.

7. Before we discipline, we need to connect first by soothing their emotional distress. Connecting helps our children become ready to listen.

8. After establishing connection, the child is now more ready to learn and you may now begin to redirect. What we want to achieve in redirecting is enabling the child to gain insight about her and other's feelings; and decide how to act upon that particular situation.

Twenty Discipline Mistakes Even Great Parents Make

As parents, we need to look and assess our own discipline strategy in order to polish our mistakes. Even the most well-informed parents can make mistakes when the No-Drama Whole-Brain discipline is disregarded, and here are some of those.

1. The main goal of discipline is to teach. However, there are parents who neglect that goal and instead divert discipline as a tool to make consequences or punishment.

2. Another mistake is thinking that being warm and loving and nurturing will only make discipline ineffective when in fact, it's the other way around.

3. We tend to be rigid instead of consistent. Keep in mind that different approaches are needed in different situations.

4. We think that discipline is a monologue-based approach when in fact, talking too much is the least effective discipline approach.

5. We tend to only see the external behavior and fail to investigate the motives or "whys" behind the behavior.

6. We tend to forget hearing our manner of talking and other nonverbal communications. It is important to remember that the manner of sending a message is as important as the message itself.

7. We tend to tell our kids how they should feel and that big emotions need to be shut off. But in fact, it is very essential to acknowledge how our children really feel.

8. We tend to overreact. It is a mistake to overreact because children become focus on our exaggerated reaction and not on their own behaviors.

9. We tend to forget the need to repair breaches. When this happens, the goal of a loving and nurturing discipline is disregarded. It is important to reconnect as it helps our children develop relational skills.

10. We tend to be emotionally reactive when in fact, we must only teach discipline when we are in a calm and receptive state.

11. We let our children soothe their big emotions on their own when in fact, they need our help in doing so.

12. We worry too much about our audience. In disciplining, it is important to focus on the child's emotions and your

emotions as well. Do not worry too much on what other people might say about your discipline approach.

13. We get confused on how to act when our children fight back. The best thing to do is give your child some break in order to find an effective resolution.

14. We base our actions with our own perspective and emotions when in fact, our children's emotions and perspective should be considered the most in order to respond effectively.

15. We tend to forget that disciplining in public is an embarrassing experience for our children. We may consider taking them to a private place first or just whispering to them. In doing so, we are showing them respect.

16. We tend to make assumptions when in fact we should give our children the chance to explain. Again, we should be flexible in all our responses.

17. We shrug off our kids' experience. No matter how silly or just of a small deal it is to us, our children's feelings are important and real to them. We need to empathize and listen closely to them.

18. We go overboard with our expectations. We expect that our children can handle themselves well and behave well at all

times but it isn't going to be the case. Remember, their brains are still developing and no matter how much we like them to behave like adults, they just can't.

19. We let our instincts be overpowered by other people's advice. Remember, our children are ours. Therefore, we must discipline them based on what we feel appropriate rather than how other people instruct us.

20. We tend to forget to be easy on ourselves. When we mess up, it is important to know that we still have plenty of chances to reconnect and make up with them.

Final Thoughts

Hey! Did you enjoy this book? We sincerely hope you thoroughly enjoyed this short read and have gotten immensely valuable insights that will help you in any areas of your life.

Would it be too greedy if we ask for a review from you?

It takes 1 minute to leave 1 review to possibly influence 1 more person's decision to read just 1 book which may change their 1 life. Your 1 minute matters and we value it and thank you so much for giving us your 1 minute. If it sucks, just say it sucks. Period.

FREE BONUS

P.S. Is it okay if we overdeliver?

Here at Abbey Beathan Publishing, we believe in overdelivering way beyond our reader's expectations. Is it okay if we overdeliver?

Here's the deal, we're going to give you an extremely valuable cheatsheet of "Accelerated Learning". We've partnered up with Ikigai Publishing to present to you the exclusive bonus of "Accelerated Learning Cheatsheet"

What's the catch? We need to trust you… You see, we want to overdeliver and in order for us to do that, we've to trust our reader to keep this bonus a secret to themselves. Why? Because we don't want people to be getting our exclusive accelerated learning cheatsheet without even buying our books itself. Unethical, right?

Ok. Are you ready?

Simply Visit this link: http://bit.ly/acceleratedcheatsheet

We hope you'll enjoy our free bonuses as much as we've enjoyed preparing it for you!

Free Bonus #2: Free Book Preview of Summary: Why Buddhism is True
The Book at a Glance

"Why Buddhism Is True: The Science and Philosophy of Meditation" is about the connections of Buddhist teachings to scientific facts about the human mind. Its main focus is on mindfulness meditation and how it can help people overcome problems and eventually attain liberation from suffering. To accomplish its goal of showing people the path towards freedom, the book gives numerous scientific studies on human psychology, testimonials from meditators such as Robert Wright himself, and helpful tips to practice Buddhist teachings in daily life. The book starts with an epigraph: an excerpt of "A Dream Play" by August Strindberg and is divided into 16 chapters about the following.

1 Taking the Red Pill

Wright describes the Buddhist tradition as similar to the red pill in the movie "The Matrix".

2 Paradoxes of Meditation

There are paradoxes in meditation and Buddhism that make sense experientially.

The formless is a Buddhist concept that causes profound insights.

11 The Upside of Emptiness

Being empty is the natural state of things; although this may seem negative, it is actually beneficial.

12 A Weedless World

Wright hates a particular kind of weed, but his meditative practices caused him to appreciate his old plant enemy.

13 Like, Wow, Everything Is One (at Most)

Hindus believe in the Oneness of everything; Buddhists believe in everything – this chapter explains why they may both be right.

14 Nirvana in a Nutshell

This chapter talks about Nirvana or enlightenment – the ultimate aspiration of Buddhists and everyone who seeks liberation.

15 Is Enlightenment Enlightening?

Chapter fifteen takes a closer look at enlightenment.

16 Meditation and the Unseen Order

The unseen order is theorized to be something that we must align ourselves into; the final chapter explains how mediation can achieve that.

Epigraph

Writer: But tell me before you go. What was the worst thing about being down here?

Agnes: Just existing. Knowing my sight was blurred by my eyes, my hearing dulled by my ears, and my bright thought trapped in the grey maze of a brain. Have you seen a brain?

Writer: And you're telling me that's what's wrong with us? How else can we be?

- A Dream Play by August Strindberg, as adapted by Caryl Churchill

A Note to Readers

Since a book with a title such as "Why Buddhism Is True" needs careful qualifications, Robert Wright sets five things clear:

1. Wright didn't discuss about the supernatural aspects of Buddhism (such as reincarnation) but only its naturalistic parts – the ideas that fit within philosophy and modern psychology. Despite this, he wants you to take Buddhism's extraordinary claims seriously because they can revolutionize how you view yourself and the world.

2. Wright focused on common fundamental ideas found across different Buddhist traditions, which vary in emphasis, doctrines, and forms.

3. Wright didn't delve into the finer parts of Buddhist philosophy and psychology.

4. Although Wright recognizes the trickiness of using the word "true" since claims of truth should be met with scepticism (this is an important lesson in

Buddhism), he believes that the word still has a place in Buddhist thought. He argues that even Buddha gave Four Noble Truths, and that Buddhism's evaluation of and remedy to the human predicament are correct, valid, and important.

5. Wright claims that asserting core Buddhist concepts' validity doesn't automatically say anything about other philosophical or spiritual traditions. He adds that there may be logical tensions between an idea in Buddhism and one from another tradition, but oftentimes there aren't any. He quotes the Dalai Lama in saying that one shouldn't try to apply what he/she learns from Buddhism to become a better Buddhist, but to become a better whatever-the-person-already-is.

CPSIA information can be obtained
at www.ICGtesting.com
Printed in the USA
BVHW041427030919
557429BV00010B/395/P